The Great Survivor
The Rebirth of a
Victorian Engine

How a Small Team of Dedicated Enthusiasts
Restored to Life an Old Steam Engine

Tim Owen

**Cumbrian
Railways
Association**

**The Furness
Railway Trust**

Contents

Acknowledgments

Funding for the project to rebuild and restore Furness Railway locomotive No. 20 was provided by:

Heritage Lottery Fund   PRISM Fund of the Science Museum
Cumbria County Council   The Idlewild Trust
Furness Building Society   Cumbrian Railways Association
                Furness Railway Trust

The author of this book received much encouragement and help in the preparation of this book and wishes to thank the following for their assistance:

Phil Cousins, Norman Gard, Geoff Holme, Peter Holmes, Fergus MacGregor and Alan Middleton.

Bibliography

Banks, A. G: *H. W. Schneider of Barrow and Bowness* (Titus Wilson, Kendal, 1984)
McGowan Gradon, W: *The Furness Railway: its Rise and Development, 1846-1923* (Altrincham, 1946)
Norman, K: *The Furness Railway* (Silver Link, 1994)
Rush, R. W: *The Furness Railway* (Oakwood Press, 1973)

Periodicals consulted:
Cumbrian Railways Association Circular: *Early Barrow Steelworks Locomotives* (Peter Holmes), May 1984
The Railway Magazine: *Furness Railway Veterans,* June 1939
Trains Illustrated: *Built to Last* (Peter Holmes), No. 52, 1984

and also:
The Iron Horse: Lakeside Railway Society

Published jointly by The Cumbrian Railways Association (Registered Charity No. 1025436)
Membership Secretary, 36 Clevelands Avenue, Barrow-in-Furness, Cumbria. LA13 0AE
and The Furness Railway Trust (Registered Charity No. 1005211)
Membership Secretary, Greystones, Mount Pleasant, Greenodd, Cumbria. LA12 7RG

Design & layout by Michael Peascod,
104 Durley Avenue, Pinner, Middlesex, HA5 1JH
Printed by Lamberts Print & Design, Settle, North Yorkshire.

ISBN 0-9519201-8-9

Introduction

THE history of Furness Railway locomotive No.20 since it was built long ago in 1863 makes a unique and fascinating story. It is all the more remarkable that the locomotive has survived at all, since it was deemed to be obsolete as a main line locomotive in 1870 when only seven years old. Since then, its fortunes have ebbed and flowed dramatically, both over its long working career of ninety-seven years and also since its retirement in 1960. Moreover, whilst it is not unheard of for railway locomotives to be altered during their working lives, FR No. 20 has been the subject of three major rebuilds and ownership has been transferred six times. Even so, having spent so many years as just another goods locomotive, out of sight of most railway enthusiasts, it was 1999 before FR No. 20 finally made the headlines, when it became the oldest standard gauge railway locomotive in Britain currently working under its own steam.

To appreciate fully how this unlikely tale came about, it is necessary to go back to 1846, when the Furness Railway Company (FRC) commenced operations over its 14 miles of track at that time isolated from the main railway network. Like many railways in northern England, the Furness Railway was conceived as a carrier of goods, the core traffic being iron ore and Furness slate, which was transported from mines notably in the Kirkby and Dalton areas to piers at Barrow. In those days, Barrow was only a small fishing hamlet, the main access from the south being the crossing of the sands of Morecambe Bay. Not surprisingly, therefore, the early locomotives purchased by the FRC had to be delivered to Barrow by sea. Fortunately, there was great demand for the rich iron ore that was the FRC's staple traffic. The railway flourished and subsequently expanded, first north to Broughton in 1848, where it was to meet the Whitehaven and Furness Junction Railway which opened in 1850, and also east from Dalton to Ulverston in 1854. Finally, a connection was made with the main rail network when the Ulverstone and Lancaster Railway was opened in 1857, this latter railway calling upon the FRC to provide the locomotives and rolling stock for its operations. The Furness Railway and the area that it served were now well and truly accessible to the rest of England. The subsequent development of tourist traffic by the FRC, together with the creation of the steel and shipbuilding industries at Barrow that were facilitated by the FRC's own entrepreneurial activities, ensured that the face of the Furness district was to change for ever.

FR No. 20 poses at Lakeside Station on the evening of Monday 21st June 1999 during trial running. A displacement lubricator has been attached to the steam chest cover, below the smokebox door, to aid lubrication of the cylinders.

Photo: Tim Owen

Above: Coppernob No. 4 in service on the Furness Railway. She was sister to the illustrious No. 3, now preserved at the National Railway Museum.   *Photo: Geoff Holme Collection.*

Below: Fairbairn 0-4-0 No. 7 of 1854, a direct development of the original **'Coppernob'***, the first type of engine used by the Furness Railway.*   *Photo: LPC Collection Ref. 46444, courtesy National Railway Museum*

1:
The Four-Wheeled Ancestors of FR No. 20

THE first motive power to be acquired by the Furness Railway came in the form of two four-wheel coupled tender locomotives which were built at the Clarence Foundry, Liverpool, of Bury, Curtis and Kennedy. Delivered in 1844, FR Nos.1 and 2 had bar frames, as distinct from the plate frames which became more commonly used in Great Britain, and a Bury's 'D'-shaped firebox having a high hemispherical dome above to create a steam space and on which two safety valves were located. This steam dome was covered in copper cladding, and the firebox was known as the 'haystack' type. Boiler working pressure was 80 pounds per square inch (psi), cylinders 13in. diameter, and driving wheels 4ft. 9in. diameter. Further details are given in the summary table at the end of the next chapter. These two locomotives were used to assist with the construction and the commissioning of the line. Two further similar locomotives were supplied by Bury, Curtis and Kennedy in 1846, coincident with the opening of the Railway, which differed from the earlier pair in having the boiler pressure increased to 110 psi and the cylinders to 14in. diameter. These two pairs of engines became Classes A1 and A2 in the (unofficial) classification system developed for Furness Railway locomotives, and hauled all the trains for the first six years of operation. Nos.1 and 2 had comparatively short working lives on the Furness Railway; No.1 was scrapped after suffering firebox damage in 1866, having been lit up at Carnforth without any water in the boiler, and No.2 was withdrawn in 1870 and sold to a colliery in Northumberland. In contrast, Nos.3 and 4 had relatively long lives, not being withdrawn until December 1898 and January 1898 respectively. No.3, which reputedly hauled the first passenger train on the Furness Railway, was well cared for and ended its days working in Barrow Docks. Known locally as *Old Coppernob* or just *Coppernob*, it was retired to a specially built ornate glass

case on the approach to Barrow Central station where it became an icon for the town of Barrow-in-Furness. *Coppernob* was removed temporarily to be exhibited at the British Empire Exhibition at London in 1924 and 1925 and was, sadly, abruptly and permanently removed after the station and the case were destroyed by a German land mine which was dropped on the night of 4th/5th May 1941. Still bearing her wartime scars, *Coppernob* is now a treasured exhibit at the National Railway Museum in York, the only remaining example of early bar-framed construction in Britain.

Bury, Curtis and Kennedy ceased manufacturing locomotives around 1850 so, when further goods locomotives were required, these were supplied by W. Fairbairn of Manchester. Fairbairns had built locomotives under contract to Bury, Curtis and Kennedy and, having acquired the necessary drawings and patterns, they were able to provide a further four 0-4-0 tender locomotives of the Bury type to the Furness Railway in 1854 and 1855. Numbered 7, 8, 9 and 10, these became Class A3 and, with the combination of an increased boiler pressure of 120 psi, cylinders of 15in. diameter, and the driving wheels reduced to 4ft. 6in., possessed a useful increase in tractive effort (i.e. pulling power). The Fairbairn engines continued to use the Bury 'haystack' firebox, but were fitted with running plates and splashers over the driving wheels.

As well as having to cope with growth in its own traffic, the Furness Railway was now called upon to supply motive power to operate both the newly opened Ulverstone and Lancaster Railway and also the Coniston Railway. Four further locomotives were supplied by Fairbairns, Nos.13 and 14 in 1858 and Nos.15 and 16 in 1861. These locomotives were designated Class A4 for, although being of generally similar dimensions to Class A3, they were fitted with a tender of the larger water capacity of 1,300 gallons instead of 1,000 gallons of the earlier class.

Another Fairbairn 0-4-0 goods engine, this time No. 13 of 1858, being closely inspected by a young man near the Strand Station in Barrow. This engine was transferred to the duplicate list in 1899 as No. 13A. It was withdrawn in 1900.
Photo: LCGB Ken Nunn Collection (Ref. H1106)

Furness Railway Co

Dec 23rd

6902.

No. 440

Gauge 4.8½.

Four Goods Engines & Tenders
Delivered in Manchester

together each £ esra net

Inside Cylinders 15½ x 24   see letter 2515.
Boiler 3.10 dia × 11.2 long.
Copper Box 3.0⅛ × 3.3¾ × 4.2½ high. H.S.   56 sq ft
141 Brass tubes 2" dia   842.75
4 wheels coupled. 4.9 dia.   Total H.S. 898.75
Wheel Base 7.9 —
Inside frames —
Two No 7 Injectors (No pumps.)
Tyres of Krupp's steel.
Axles. piston rod & Crank pins &c.

Tender on 4 wheels   to contain 1200 gallons
Tyres solid rolled. J. Brown Rotherham.
Axles of Krupp's cast steel.
Brake to act on both sides of each wheel.
280] Bourdon's Pressure Gauge.
   2 Engines & Tenders to be delivered in May 1863

RC 24/12

1 Del Aug 1st 1863. 1 del Aug 6/63.
1 Del " 10th 63. 1 " " 2/63.

The page from the Sharp, Stewart order book giving details of Order No. 440 for four 0-4-0 tender goods engines. Set out on the page is a rather detailed description of the engines, and this page, with the drawings, would be the starting point of the construction of the engines destined for the Furness Railway. The line struck across the page presumably denotes the fact that the order had been fulfilled.

Courtesy: Mitchell Library

2:
The Sharp, Stewart 0-4-0 Tender Locomotives

OUTPUT of iron ore from the Furness mines had developed rapidly, rising from 100,000 tons in the mid-1840s to 700,000 tons by 1864. In 1859, the Furness Railway had the foresight to lease land at Hindpool, in Barrow, to the firm of Schneider, Hannay & Co. in order to establish an ironworks which, by 1862, had seven blast furnaces in operation. The invention of the Bessemer process for the production of steel also had a significant impact on the Furness district in that the rich ores were ideal for steel production. 1864 saw the formation of the Barrow Haematite Steel Co. Ltd., which commenced construction of a steel works in order to exploit the Bessemer process and to make best use of the high quality haematite pig iron close at hand. The Barrow Haematite Steel Co. Ltd. (BHSCo.) subsequently bought out the mines and ironworks of Schneider, Hannay & Co. and emerged, reputedly, as the largest producer of iron and steel in the world.

The development of the iron and steel industry had been aided by the entrepreneurial assistance of the FRC and its Directors, who then not only benefited from carrying the increased production from the mines, but also the finished iron and steel. Not surprisingly, therefore, the 1860s saw a phenomenal increase in the Furness Railway's locomotive fleet which, in 1861, stood at a total of only 16.

Whilst the Stockton & Darlington Railway had been using six-wheeled coupled locomotives as long ago as the mid 1840s, the Furness Railway had continued to remain loyal to the 0-4-0 configuration that was to serve it well for

over fifty years. The 0-4-0s were eminently suitable for accessing the many sidings which served the mines, the lifeblood of the Railway. Richard Mason, who took over from James Ramsden as Locomotive Superintendent in 1850, was known to hold them in high regard, and woe betide anyone who questioned their ability.

When the FRC decided that it required a further four locomotives, it is not surprising that they stayed with the 0-4-0 tender configuration and turned to Sharp, Stewart & Co. of Manchester, who had not only taken over much of the Fairbairn business but, as Sharp, Brothers, had also earlier supplied the Furness Railway with four passenger tank locomotives. So it was that, on 23rd December 1862, a batch of four 0-4-0 tender locomotives, to Sharp, Stewart's own design, was ordered. Gone, however, were the bar frames and the 'haystack' firebox, to be replaced by wrought iron plate frames and a rectangular round-topped firebox. Cylinder diameter was increased to $15^{1}/_{2}$in. and driving wheel diameter to 4ft. 9in., surprisingly large, perhaps, for what was to be primarily a goods locomotive. With a boiler pressure of 120 psi, this combination gave a tractive effort of 10,317 lbs.

The extract from the Sharp, Stewart (SS) order book, reproduced opposite, shows the boiler to be to the standard SS diameter of 3ft. 10in. and 11ft. 2in. long, with a copper firebox and 141 brass tubes of 2in. diameter. This was to give a total heating surface of 898.75 square feet. The engine's tyres and axles, piston rods and crank pins, along with the tender tyres, were to be of Krupp's steel. The

This fine study of locomotive No. 27 formed a prime reference document for the development of plans for the reconstruction of BHSCo. No. 7. Taken in Barrow Yard, note the bowler-hatted gentleman by the cab steps. He is thought to be a railway employee charged with the task of looking after the photographer.

Photo: LPC Collection Ref. 14639, courtesy National Railway Museum

A later photograph of the Furness Railway 0-4-0 good engine No. 28. It will be noted that the number plate has been moved from the boiler to the cab side-sheets. This was done in about 1896 Photo: LCGB Ken Nunn Collection (Ref. H1095)

order, No.440, also states that the first two locomotives were to be delivered in May 1863. The drawings for the engine (SS 1028) and tender (SS 1218) were both signed off by a Mr. Bottomley, the latter being clearly dated April 22nd 1863. It is not surprising to see, therefore, that all four locomotives (SS Nos. *1434, 1435, 1447* and *1448*) were not delivered until August 1863, on the 1st, 6th, 10th and 21st. They were numbered 17, 18, 19 and 20 respectively in the Furness Railway fleet and were recorded in the capital account ledger of the Furness Railway at a total cost of £9,641 5s 2d. This equates to £2,410.31 each in decimal currency.

The FRC subsequently ordered two further batches of two locomotives each, which were delivered in 1865 (SS Nos. *1585* and *1586*) and 1866 (SS Nos. *1663* and *1664*). These were almost identical in design but, apparently, possessed fireboxes which were 3in. longer. The engines were typically Victorian in their design, with a high bell-mouthed dome, housing the regulator valve and Salter safety valves, situated on the front boiler ring. The wheel splashers were embellished with curved brass strips, but there was still no cab, the only protection being afforded by a small curved weatherboard. The engines were characterised by a deep valance that ran from the front buffer beam and which curved downwards to form the steps at the rear. Stephenson

Link valve gear was employed, the throw of the reversing shaft, and the consequent rise and fall of the expansion link, being counteracted by a spiral torsion spring attached to the frame of the engine.

The tenders had a capacity of 1,200 gallons and 2 tons of coal and were of the same basic design that was to be delivered with the many larger locomotives from Sharp, Stewart in later years. The tenders of the 0-4-0 locomotives are distinguished by the slightly lower footplate area, which curves down from the coal space behind. The tenders delivered to the FRC were notable for the box at the back of the water tank, which probably contained re-railing jacks. The only brakes on the locomotive were located on the tender and applied by hand.

In 1866, the FRC ordered a further four of the four-coupled design, to be numbered 29 - 32, but this order was subsequently cancelled in favour of Class D1 0-6-0 tender locomotives; instead 1866 saw the arrival of the first of 55 of these successful locomotives which were supplied by Sharp, Stewart over a period of 18 years. These, with an increased weight and tractive effort of 11,605 lbs, were more suited to the heavier trains required by the rapid growth in freight traffic, and this led to an early end to main line operations for six of the Class A5 locomotives.

Comparative Details of the FR 'A' Class 0-4-0 Locomotives

Class	Cylinders Dia x Stroke inches	Steam Pressure psi	Driving Wheels ft-ins	Weight Engine tons	Tender tons	Tractive Effort lbs
A1	13 x 24	80	4-9	17.75	12.9	5,443
A2	14 x 24	110	4-9	19.5	12.9	7,617
A3	15 x 24	120	4-6	21.5	15.6	9,350
A4	15 x 24	120	4-6	24.2	17.7	9,350
A5	15$^{1}/_{2}$ x 24	120	4-9	24.9	19.75	10,317

3:
A Second Life for the Sharp, Stewart 0-4-0s

One of the former Furness Railway class A5 engines poses with staff at Park Mines in about 1880 after transfer to the Barrow Haematite Steel Co. Ltd. The engine has been rebuilt as a saddle tank locomotive.

Photo: Cumbria County Record Office, Barrow (Ref. BDP37)

THE iron and steelworks at Barrow now occupied a considerable acreage at their Hindpool site, with large sidings to accommodate inwards and outwards traffic. In addition, there was a need to transport raw materials and finished goods around the site and also to dispose of the resulting slag to the banks that grew up nearby on the seaward side.

The BHSCo. had already acquired a small fleet of 0-4-0 saddle-tank locomotives, built by Neilson and Sharp, Stewart. The expanding production of iron and steel was obviously placing increased pressure on its motive power and a further 0-4-0ST, of 14in. cylinder diameter, was ordered from Sharp, Stewart in 1870, SS order No. 576. This order was, however, promptly cancelled when the decision was taken by the BHSCo. to purchase six of the FRC's Class A5 locomotives at a cost of £1,550 each.

The sale by the FRC of these relatively new locomotives appears to have stemmed from the rapidly increasing freight traffic which demanded larger and more powerful 0-6-0 locomotives. The earlier 0-4-0s were still capable of handling the short trip workings and shunting duties, so it was felt commercially expedient to sell the Sharp, Stewart 0-4-0s whilst they still attracted a good second-hand price. The fact that Nos. 27 and 28 soldiered on with the Furness Railway for a career extending to 52 years suggests that there was nothing wrong with the design of the locomotive.

The sale was authorised in a Directors' minute of the FRC dated 25th May 1870. With hindsight, there can be no surprise that such a transfer of locomotives between the two companies should take place, for the Board of the

BHSCo. contained the names of James Ramsden and the Duke of Devonshire, who were both directors of the FRC which, itself, had shares in the BHSCo. It is interesting to note that the order by the FRC for replacement Class D1 0-6-0 locomotives was allocated the next consecutive SS order, No. 577, to that of the 0-4-0 order.

There is still a deal of mystery surrounding the timing of the transfers of the Class A5 locomotives, and also the re-numbering of the locomotives within the BHSCo. fleet. It is believed that FR Nos. 17-20 were transferred in 1870, and this is backed up by the arrival that year of the replacement Class D1s, which were numbered 17-20. It is also assumed that Class A5 Nos. 25 and 26 were not transferred to the BHSCo. until 1873, when a further two replacement Class D1 locomotives arrived to take up their respective numbers in the FR fleet.

These assumptions are reinforced by the Board minutes of 25th May 1870 and 19th February 1872 which specifically refer to the replacement locomotives being purchased without tenders at estimated costs of £2,000 (1870) and £2,005 (1872). The loss on the sale of the locomotives to the BHS Co., at £450, was relatively small considering the seven years of service that they had already given to the Furness Railway and indicated that it was an astute move by the board of the FRC.

Even more doubt has surrounded the actual numbers allocated to each of the former FR locomotives within the BHSCo. fleet. For many years, in the absence of any other evidence, it was assumed that the following identities were taken up by the FR engines:

SS No.	FR No.	BHSCo.No.	Transfer Date
1434	17	5	1870
1435	18	7	1870
1447	19	8	1870
1448	20	16	1870
1585	25	17	1873
1586	26	18	1873

Although there appears to be no evidence to substantiate this alignment of the fleet numbers, the assumption that the BHSCo. numbers were allocated in exactly the same order as the former FR fleet numbers seems to have gained considerable credence, and various directories of rolling stock published over the years have quoted the numbering system above. As the reader will find out later in this book, the above assumptions were found to be flawed when, in 1998, the Furness Railway Trust revealed that conclusive evidence had been found that BHSCo. No.7 (the prime subject of this publication) had been built as SS No.*1448*. This indicated that it had, in fact, been Furness Railway No.20, and not FR No.18 as shown above. Similar evidence, however, confirmed that BHSCo. No.17 was indeed SS *1585* and, therefore, FR No. 25 as previously assumed.

All of the BHSCo. fleet of former Furness Railway Class A5 locomotives were re-built to saddle-tank configuration upon transfer. It is fairly certain that this conversion was undertaken by Sharp, Stewart, rather than the BHSCo. itself. There is only one known photograph of the initial re-build, reproduced here courtesy of the Barrow Record Office. This shows that the basic Sharp, Stewart lines were retained, the loss of the tender water capacity being partially offset by the addition of a flat sided tank, which largely obscured the bell mouthed dome and caused the Salter safety valve arrangement to be re-arranged at an angle of ninety degrees so that the springs were attached to the side of the tank. The locomotives kept their original chimney and smokebox, but their classic lines were, again, mainly degraded by the new tank. At the rear, the weather board was retained, although the cab sides appear to have been moved outwards in order to allow the driver to see around the new saddle tank.

Most of the saddle-tank locomotives were subsequently rebuilt again during their careers with the BHSCo. and received replacement wheels of 4ft. 0in. diameter, more suitable to their works environment and giving them increased tractive effort. BHSCo. No.7 was, however, an exception in that, whilst it underwent an extensive rebuild in 1915, it retained its larger 4ft. 9in. wheels, making it something of an oddity within the BHSCo fleet. The appearance of No.7 was again substantially altered in the 1915 rebuild. A new 120 psi boiler was fitted, having a smaller dome on the centre ring, and with new Ramsbottom safety valves located above the firebox. A new curved tank was fitted and the deep valances removed, although the original splashers and even the Furness Railway style front upper lamp bracket were retained. At last, a cab was fitted for the protection of the crew, and new Gresham and Craven injectors were fitted, replacing the original Gifford injectors. The engine also gained a new and squatter chimney, more in keeping with an industrial saddle-tank, as well as new sand boxes. The springs and spring hangers had probably already been altered in order to accommodate the additional weight of the saddle-tank; the weight of the engine after the 1915 alterations stood at 36 tons compared with only 25 tons when it was built in 1863.

Barrow Haematite Steel Co. No. 5 is seen on the railbank at the steelworks in the 1920s.

Photo: Dock Museum, Barrow

The rebuild was undertaken at the BHSCo.'s own workshops, which had extensive facilities. The BHSCo. was also known to have undertaken major overhauls, and, through subsequent overhauls, had increased the diameter of the cylinders to 16in. from 15½in. using its own boring machine, reputedly copied from one owned by the Furness Railway. Consequently, the tractive effort was raised by 6.5% from 10,317 lbs to 10,995 lbs.

The prime duties of the other former FR engines included regular assaults on the zig-zag incline up the slag banks. However, particularly during its early years with the BHSCo., No.7 was usually allocated the job of moving the hot metal wagons from the blast furnaces to the Mixer, a large gas-heated storage reservoir for molten pig iron, situated at the North end of the ironworks. The purpose of the Mixer was to provide a constant supply of pig iron for steelmaking by compensating for any irregularity in the working of the blast furnaces, and also to give a more uniform composition to the iron by combining the pig iron from several furnaces. A railway line ran in a tunnel along the front of the furnaces, beneath the casting beds, and the hot metal wagons were positioned along this line according to which furnaces were next to cast. No.7, with its larger wheelsets and consequent enhanced speed, would then quickly move the hot pig iron to the Mixer before too much heat had been lost.

The former Furness Railway saddle-tanks were not, apparently, wholly restricted to the confines of the Hindpool site. At least two (No.5 and probably No.17) were known to have been located at Park Mines for a long period of time. In Barrow, it was common for the BHSCo. locos to haul pig iron from the works past the Devonshire and Buccleuch Docks along to Ramsden Dock. The June 1939 edition of Railway Magazine, which includes a picture of No.7, records that the former Furness Railway locomotives were capable of hauling 45 loaded pig iron wagons, and local accounts suggest that these game little saddle-tanks were capable of putting up a good show as they buckled down to their task on their former FR stamping ground.

Another crossroads in the career of No.7 loomed with the nationalisation and transfer of the steelworks to the Ministry of Supply in 1942. With the split due to take place on 31st October, the BHSCo., not surprisingly, conducted a review of its locomotive fleet, and a summary was produced by the Engineer's Office dated 26th October 1942. This makes interesting reading, recording that there were 20 locomotives in the fleet, 13 of which were in commission, 6 on standby, and one on loan. The report picked out the eight best locomotives, of which five were retained by the BHSCo. No.7 was not viewed as being in good condition and was, consequently, passed over to the Ministry of Supply. The report read:

Loco 7: Boiler constructed 1915. The landings of the copper firebox are fractured and leaking very badly. We can only do a temporary repair from time to time as there is very little landing left near to the rivets. In the event of it leaking too badly, it would need a new firebox. This boiler has not been welded - and up to the present, no sign of any throat or front plate fracture are shewing.

Despite the problems outlined above, No.7 continued to work within the steelworks complex until the end of steam working in 1960. Photographs taken during the 1950s show that the spokes had become curved over time, which speaks volumes for the hard work that it had endured during its long working life. Even at this late stage, No.7 must have been thought worthy of further investment, for the wheels had been renewed by the time that the locomotive had been officially withdrawn from traffic on 8th July 1960. Some other work must also have been undertaken, for examination of photographs shows that the positions of the injectors were altered between 1953 and 1959.

Nos. 7 and 17 were the last of the former Furness Railway veterans to remain in service, both of them at the Steelworks. There must have been some degree of affection for them as they were both fated to avoid the cutter's torch, being afforded retirement to local schools.

No.7 was removed to the George Hastwell School in Barrow on 29th September 1960, and No. 17 was taken to the Stonecross Special School at Ulverston the same month. The Steelworks obviously wanted to give these loyal servants a good send off, and some effort was expended in ensuring that they were both complete and spruced up before they were transported to their new homes. This was most fortuitous in the light of future events.

No. 7 seen at Barrow Steelworks on 15th April 1953. Note the curved spokes, particularly on the rear driving wheels. These wheels were replaced before the locomotive was retired by the steelworks in 1960

Photo: Frank Jones.

4:

Retirement

NO.7 quickly became a local landmark at its new home in Abbey Road, Barrow-in-Furness. Over the years, many children played on the old engine as it sat there in the grounds of the George Hastwell School, and a generation grew up as it weathered the seasons in its retirement. Similarly, No.17 led a more secluded life near Ulverston, its wheels embedded in concrete on a short stretch of track. As with most things, time and the elements started to cause deterioration and, with the demise of steam on the national rail network in 1968, it became all the more important that these historic locomotives were given a secure future.

The Lakeside Railway Society (LRS), formed in 1968 out of the old Lancashire Railway Circle to support the re-opening of the branchline from Plumpton Junction (near Ulverston) to Lakeside, was aware of these engines and, as early as 1970, established contact with the Head of the Stonecross School, who eventually agreed that No.17 could be taken to Haverthwaite. However, the more pressing need to assist with the preparations to re-open the Lakeside & Haverthaite Railway (L&HR) caused this move to be put to one side. The initiative was brought to a permanent halt in 1974 when the L&HR was transferred out of Lancashire into the new County of Cumbria. In the meantime, No.17 had been taken under the wing of Lancashire County Museums.

It was to be 1983 before there was a successful initiative to disturb these locomotives from their slumber. Ian Atkinson, then General Manager of Steamtown Railway Museum, and Lance Wooff joined forces to purchase No.7 and it was transported from Barrow to Carnforth on 29th November 1983. Shortly afterwards it was agreed that Ian and Lance should be given custody of No. 17, which re-joined No.7 at the very edge of Furness Railway territory.

Attention was immediately focussed on No.7 which was, over a short period of time, stripped down in order to enable restoration to commence. The intention was to return No.7 to its 1863 configuration as a tender locomotive, but the initiative was to fail through the untimely death of Lance and Ian's resignation from Carnforth.

As might be imagined, the Lakeside Railway Society had kept in close touch with the above events, and had been supportive of the initiative to return No.7 to her former glory as a tender locomotive. This interest was then rewarded with the option to purchase the dismantled remains of No.7 and, given the unfortunate events that had given rise to the sale, the deal was completed quickly and with little publicity.

The purchase price of £5,000 was raised through donations by a number of LRS stalwarts who believed it vital that such an important artefact should be retained in the Furness area which it had served so well. It has to be said that their foresight was not applauded by all at Haverthwaite, for the Society had already embarked upon the ambitious task of returning to steam the former Great Western Railway 0-6-2T locomotive No.5643, the purchase of which in 1987 had already strained the Society's finances. However, such rancour was forgotten over time and the purchase inspired the Society's Committee to increase its efforts to create a charitable body which could take on board such restoration projects and attract grants and tax concessions. It was on 25th October 1991 that the Furness Railway Trust (FRT) was finally awarded charitable status, the first important step in the long road to restoring No.7 once more to steamable condition.

No. 7 is the centre of attention from local school children during its retirement in the grounds of the George Hastwell School, Abbey Road, Barrow-in-Furness. Photo: Ken Royall

5:

Plans are Laid

THE swift nature of the purchase of No.7 meant that it was some time before it sank into everyone's minds what exactly had been bought. With the locomotive now well and truly in many pieces, efforts were immediately made to trace photographs of No.7 in service, both as a saddle-tank and in its former guise as a tender locomotive. Of course, in those days the Furness Railway Trust believed that it had actually acquired Furness Railway No.18 but, whilst it was relatively easy to obtain prints of No.7 in service with the BHSCo. and the steelworks, not a single photograph could be found of Class A5 No.18, nor, for that matter, of any of the other Class A5 locomotives destined for the BHSCo. Fortunately, the last two Class A5 locomotives, Nos. 27 and 28, remained with the FRC in almost original condition until being scrapped in 1918. Even so, the Trust has only managed to trace four photographs, two each of Nos. 27 and 28. Fortunately, what was lacking in quantity was more than made up for in quality with the National Railway Museum's $8\frac{1}{2}$in. x $6\frac{1}{2}$in. glass negative of No.27 taken at Barrow in the 1880s. Rivet detail was clearly visible as was, under magnification, the level of the water in the single gauge glass.

The Summer 1990 edition of the Lakeside Railway Society's journal, *The Iron Horse*, contained an article by Norman Gard which summarised the knowledge gained of the locomotive at that time and outlined plans for the future. In fact, there was never any doubt amongst members that the Trust should attempt to continue with the aspirations of Ian Atkinson and Lance Wooff and transform the engine back to its 1863 condition. However, the initial rose-tinted estimate of £45,000 subsequently proved to be far short of the mark. Perhaps that was just as well for, if the actual final cost had been known at that time, it might have subdued the Trust's enthusiasm to take the project on board.

One of the first actions taken by the Trust was to instigate a full professional examination of the engine's boiler and firebox. This was conducted by the L&HR's boiler inspector, Jerry Bayley, and concluded that these components had, effectively, reached the end of their working lives. Whilst the condemnation of such a substantial part of the engine could easily have been seen as a major setback to the project, it must be remembered that the original boiler and firebox had been replaced in 1915, and this had significantly altered the appearance of the locomotive. The requirement to manufacture a third new boiler and firebox for No.7 opened the way for the original 1863 outline design to be specified, with the large dome positioned on the front boiler ring behind the chimney.

Another important task was to find and identify the many components of the engine that had, by now, become scattered around the site at Carnforth. These were, as far as possible, gathered together, an inventory prepared, and some initial cleaning undertaken. Piecing together a locomotive that you have not been involved in dismantling is always a tricky task, but this was helped by the presence at Carnforth of BHSCo. No.17 which, fortunately, was still intact.

Spirits were boosted by the tracing of the original outline Sharp, Stewart general arrangement drawings for order No. 440, which were held at the Science Museum in London. These were to prove invaluable in the FRT's quest to restore No.7 to its original condition, and it enabled a start to be made on the outline boiler specification. The plans also revealed that, on conversion to a saddle-tank, alterations had been made to the valve gear of the engine, with the reversing shaft and lifting links having been inverted, and the spiral torsion compensating spring replaced by a balance weight.

Loading No. 7 onto a lowloader at George Hastwell Special School in November 1983 for the journey to Steamtown Carnforth.
Photo: North West Evening Mail

With the Trust's main attention still being focused on the restoration of former GWR 0-6-2T locomotive No.5643, there still seemed little chance of making significant physical progress on No.7 especially if it required expenditure of any degree. Nevertheless, it was also clear that the longer No.7 remained at Carnforth as an incomplete jigsaw, still largely exposed to the elements, the more unlikely it would be that the dream of seeing it steam again in any shape or form would be realised.

The Trust was, therefore, more than glad to receive the offer of funding for initial exploratory and remedial work to the frames of the engine, which were moved to the Longridge workshops of Victoria Engineering on 15th June 1993. Here it was possible to remove broken and damaged studs and, more importantly, examine the rear frames and drag box to discover how these had been altered on the conversion from tender locomotive to saddle-tank. Plans for a new drag box were drawn up by Norman Gard and some initial work to enable conversion back to a tender locomotive undertaken.

Shortage of space at Longridge and a lack of any further imminent funding on the horizon meant that the frames had to be placed once again into storage, and so they were transported to a private site at Lytham on 17th June 1995. However, the preparatory work had enabled detailed measurements of the frames to be taken and enabled a fuller understanding to be gained of the restoration work that would be required to put the locomotive back into 1863 condition.

Meanwhile, plans were afoot in the Furness area for celebrations in 1996 to mark the 150th anniversary of the Furness Railway. In February 1995 Peter van Zeller, a leading member of the Cumbrian Railways Association (CRA) and well known driver on the Ravenglass & Eskdale Railway, approached the FRT with the offer of assistance in completing applications for grant aid, which he believed could be made available for the restoration of No.7 He believed that the proposed celebrations offered an unrepeatable opportunity to gain financial support for the project.

Following a meeting of interested parties in May 1994, attended by the FRT, Furness and Cartmel Tourism had employed a consultant to prepare a feasibility study for what was to become known as *Furness 150*; this was published in April 1995 and was supportive of the return to steam of FR No.18 during the celebrations in 1996. Nevertheless, it was apparent to the FRT that, despite the enthusiasm of those organisations associated with the proposed celebrations, there was no obvious short-cut to gaining sponsorship for the project. Although timescales decreed that it was now very unlikely that the locomotive would be in steam for August 1996, there was still considerable benefit to be gained in utilising the celebrations as a catalyst for attracting funding for the project; as a start, a formal application was made to the PRISM Fund of the Science Museum for a grant.

The initial response from the PRISM Fund was that it would be prepared to consider awarding a grant for the conservation of the original chassis, but would not be prepared to support financially the construction of a new boiler and tender. This, though, was a fruitful start and a small working party consisting of Trust Chairman, Tim Owen, and committee members Alan Middleton and Fergus MacGregor prepared detailed costings for the restoration of the engine chassis on a commercial basis. The PRISM Fund's requirements for the costs for all items of work to be analysed between labour and materials enforced a discipline that was to be followed later for the engine's superstructure, boiler and tender.

It was 12th January 1996 when confirmation of the award of a grant of £10,768 was sent by the PRISM Fund to the FRT, based on a total estimated cost of £34,790 for restoring the engine's chassis. This was tremendous news and marked the real beginning of the project. Work intensified on the completion of an application to the Heritage Lottery Fund for a grant of £105,000 towards the total cost, which was now estimated at £130,000. This was despatched on 2nd March with a special request that any approval be granted in time for the main *Furness 150* celebrations on 24th August 1996.

6:

Furness Railway 150

ALTHOUGH scaled down from original aspirations, a full programme of events had been drawn up for the celebrations to commemorate the 150th Anniversary of the opening of the Furness Railway in 1846. The Furness Railway Trust had already responded positively to a request to repaint its 0-6-0ST 'Austerity' locomotive into Furness Railway Indian Red livery, and the re-entry into service of the locomotive after overhaul had acted as the centrepiece for the commencement of the celebrations on 24th August 1995.

The FRT's project team for the restoration of BHSCo. No.7 was also instrumental in writing and performing a musical documentary on the Furness Railway entitled *The Iron Road*, which was performed at a number of venues formerly served by the Furness Railway and was also broadcast on local radio. Several new songs were written for the project including, inevitably, the story of FR No.18.

The celebrations would not have been complete without an appearance of Barrow's favourite steam locomotive i.e. Furness Railway No.3 *Coppernob*. Arrangements were made for her to be transported on a low loader from the National Railway Museum at York on Friday 16th August so that she could be displayed the following day at her former resting place on Barrow Station and then at Ulverston before proceeding to Haverthwaite where she would stay for ten days. *Coppernob* would then be the

focus of the *Furness 150* celebrations at Haverthwaite on Saturday, 24th August, the exact anniversary of the first Furness Railway passenger train in 1846 and the highlight of the programmed events.

Nerves were now beginning to be stretched for a number of reasons. First of all, the time was now fast approaching when the Heritage Lottery Fund was due to announce its make or break decision as to whether it would provide funding for the Class A5 project. Secondly, there were some last minute worries as to whether a road transporter could be found that would be low enough to take *Coppernob* under the Leeman Road railway bridge in York.

However, Friday, 16th August saw a small party from Furness gather at the National Railway Museum promptly at 8.00 am to assist in the loading of *Coppernob*. To say that all did not go smoothly that day would be something of an understatement. First of all, *Coppernob*'s low slung cylindrical shaped ashpan fouled the end of the transporter when loading up. Then *Coppernob* tried to derail herself on the ramp, which caused a temporary halt to operations whilst she was jacked back into place. Finally, it was necessary for the transporter to make an unscheduled turn against the flow of traffic in a one way section which caused temporary gridlock in the centre of York. Unbeknown to those concerned, the whole episode was being monitored by police on closed circuit

Coppernob at Haverthwaite, Sunday 25th August 1996. A theatrical smoke generator was used for this photographic evening.
Photo: Tim Owen

15

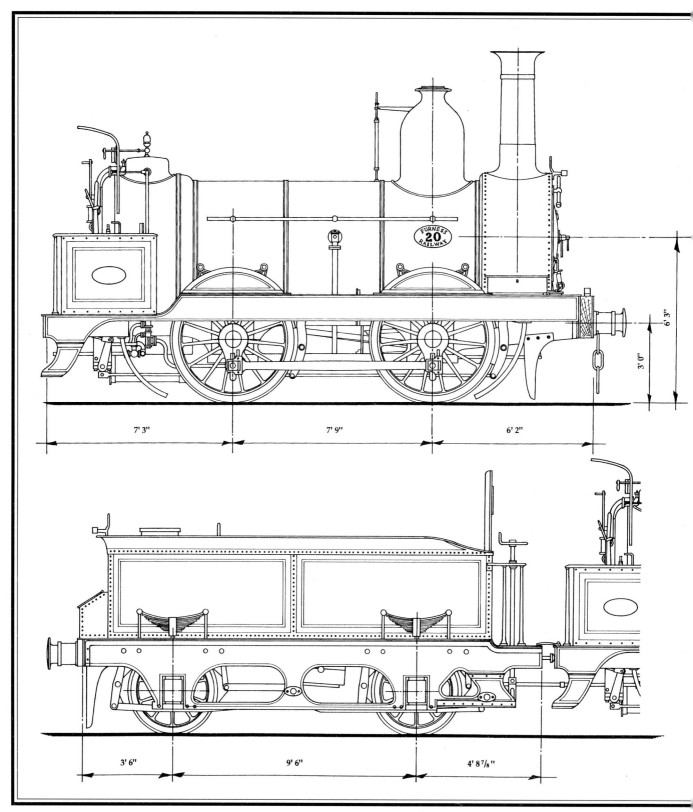

television and led to the notorious headline 'Traffic Police Nab Our Train' in the following day's *North West Evening Mail*!

Despite these unforeseen tribulations, *Coppernob*'s arrival in Furness was greeted with unimagined adulation. Large crowds gathered at Barrow Station, and people who remembered her standing proudly there before the bomb in 1941 came even in their wheelchairs to touch her. In Ulverston the town band played *See The Conquering Hero Comes* and *Will Ye No Come Back Again* to welcome home Furness's long lost hero. *Coppernob* then proceeded to

Haverthwaite Station where she would spend the remainder of her fortnight's vacation away from the National Railway Museum. Her arrival in Furness inevitably stirred up local feelings and the following week found some pressure in the local press for *Coppernob* to come home on a permanent basis. Or could a replacement be conjured up?

The Heritage Lottery Fund had indicated that the application for grant would take five months to process, which meant that the FRT could expect a decision at the beginning of August. It was true to its promise, and the author was informed that the project would be considered at

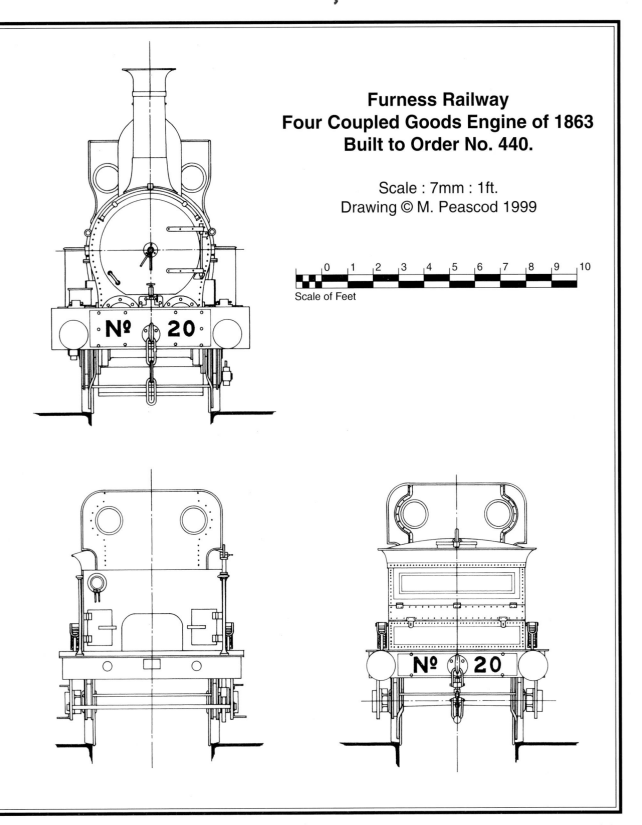

**Furness Railway
Four Coupled Goods Engine of 1863
Built to Order No. 440.**

Scale : 7mm : 1ft.
Drawing © M. Peascod 1999

Scale of Feet

a meeting of the HLF Trustees on 13th August. In the afternoon of that day, a telephone call was received from the HLF, but the line immediately went dead. After a seemingly interminable length of time (actually 20 minutes), the news came that the HLF was prepared to make a grant of £97,500, i.e.75%, towards the total cost of £130,000. Would the FRT be prepared to go forward on that basis? Although £7,500 short of the FRT's original request, there was no going back now and the HLF was very cooperative in agreeing to the news being broken on the planned date, 24th August.

The ceremony to mark the 150th Anniversary of the first Furness Railway passenger train took place at Barrow station when a commemorative plaque was unveiled in the presence of the Mayors of Barrow, Copeland, Dalton and Ulverston. The author, as master of ceremonies on behalf of North West Regional Railways, was able to break the news that Furness was at last to have a permanent replacement for *Coppernob*. The timing of the announcement could not have been better and the news received widespread media coverage.

7:

Back Home to Barrow

Whilst obtaining funding had, up until now, been the FRT Committee's main priority, attention had also been directed to the important task of finding suitable facilities to accommodate the locomotive during the restoration process. Workshops with the necessary experience and equipment to re-build steam locomotives do exist, although they are few and far between in Britain today. However, this was not to be a straightforward overhaul, requiring a strip down and re-assembly using most of the original components. The engine had already been dismantled and was to be re-constructed differently, with new components being integrated into the locomotive alongside careful conservation of existing material. Considerable input would be required from FRT personnel to manage the project and there was, therefore, a strong requirement for it to be based as close as possible to the South Lakes area.

Both logic and sentiment suggested that the Barrow-in-Furness workshops of Vickers Shipbuilding & Engineering Ltd (VSEL), later to become known as Marconi Marine (Barrow), would be an ideal choice as it had extensive engineering workshops and facilities.

Although a little reticent at first to get involved with a project that was not within its direct line of business, 'Vickers' (as it has long been known to the inhabitants of Furness) came forward with an extremely helpful offer to undertake the work in line with the costings that had been submitted to the HLF.

This, however, would not be the first time that railway work had been undertaken during the shipyard's long history. After the First World War had taken a heavy toll on the maintenance of the nation's railway rolling stock, a number of major overhauls on steam locomotives were undertaken by Vickers in the very building where FR 18 was to be resurrected. At around the same time, Vickers also took on board the rebuilding of a batch of electric locomotives for London's Metropolitan Railway. Later, in the 1960s, Vickers was again heavily involved in the railway business, this time in connection with the construction of Sulzer engines, under licence, for a variety of British Railways diesel electric locomotives. Finally, it had, in 1978, undertaken a well publicised overhaul of the world famous steam locomotive, *Flying Scotsman*.

"Here comes Coppernob!" ('Vickers shipyard to take on 0-4-0 rebuild')

Courtesy: John Hart

Vickers Works in Barrow-in-Furness were no strangers to locomotive work. Illustrated on the facing page are examples of earlier projects.
Top: London & North Western Railway 4-6-0 tender locomotive No. 1328, built in 1908, is pictured after the First World War on the Gun Shop crane, close to where FR No. 20 was restored.   Photo: Ken Norman Collection

Bottom: World famous London & North Eastern Railway 'Pacific' locomotive No. 4472 **Flying Scotsman** *was overhauled by VSEL in 1978. It is seen here being lifted by the 250 tons capacity crane alongside Devonshire Dock*
Photo: Marconi Marine

8:

Restoration Commences - 1996

THE FRT finally concluded the grant contract with the HLF on 8th October, and only at that point could work on the locomotive commence. The project was to have a timescale of two years. One of the first jobs was to finalise a contract for the construction of a new boiler and firebox. Whilst preparing estimates for the grant bid, FRT had taken the opportunity to find and assess likely suppliers which could meet the outline specification already prepared. The firm of Israel Newton & Sons of Bradford had previously undertaken satisfactory work for the Ravenglass and Eskdale Railway and had provided realistic quotes for both a welded and a riveted boiler. After some consultation and debate, the Trust opted for a boiler and firebox of mainly riveted construction from Israel Newton on the basis that, not only was it more in keeping with the 1863 built engine, but also because there was far more experience of operating railway locomotives with boilers

of this type of manufacture. Interestingly, the reduced need for weld testing during construction resulted in the riveted boiler being slightly cheaper.

It was now important to round up the engine frames, wheels and other components as soon as possible and get them into the shipyard. November saw three pallet loads of the engine's motion delivered to VSEL's Engine Shop in Barrow, followed by the frames, cylinder covers and brake rigging on 18th December. There, in the massive 19th century building, No.7 joined naval guns under overhaul and state of the art components for the Trident submarine fleet. By now, the project had been broken down into 120 separately costed work packages, so the opportunity was taken to label each part of the motion delivered to Barrow with its respective job code to assist VSEL's staff in identification. At last, the project was well and truly on its way, and the Trust now looked forward optimistically to the year ahead.

Where do you start? Some of the parts of No. 7 were dispersed over a wide area at Steamtown Carnforth. An early task was to locate them and make an inventory.

Photo: Alan Middleton

9:

Getting Down to Work - 1997

THE project manager at VSEL, Neil Johnson, decided almost immediately that the frames would benefit from light sand blasting to remove the many years of paint and dirt, and this was achieved just in time for an important and successful visit on 21st January 1997 by the PRISM Fund Manager, Simon Chaplin, who was satisfied with the way that the project was proceeding.

The FRT had, by that time, also made contact with life member Jon Wilkinson, who had been a prominent volunteer at Haverthwaite in the early days of preservation. Jon was now a manager within the nuclear safety section at VSEL and his welcome offer to assist the project 'from the inside' was readily accepted by Neil; Jon's deep knowledge and experience of steam locomotives, as well as his network of contacts within VSEL, proved over time to be extremely beneficial. Jon's first task was to ensure that the sand blasting process did not damage the cylinders and valve chest.

Before transfer back from the sand blasting booth to the Engine Shop, where the locomotive was to be restored, the opportunity was taken to give the frames a protective coat of red oxide. It was some time after this that the author received a telephone call from Jon that was, eventually, to provide one of the biggest talking points of the project. During an examination of the frames, Jon had come across some numerals stamped upon the slide bar support brackets riveted to the frames. The coating of red oxide now clearly highlighted these numerals which, uniformly, proclaimed the number *1448*. Did this mean anything to the Trust? It took only a minute or so to confirm that this was in fact the Sharp, Stewart works number for Furness Railway locomotive No.20. Alan Middleton confirmed that he had also spotted the number *1448* on some of the motion, although he had also found one instance of the expected number for FR No.18, i.e.*1435*, on the left hand big end strap.

At last, it appeared that an important mystery had been solved, but, before the news was broadcast to the world, it was important to be absolutely sure of the facts. With no urgency to declare its hand on the matter, the few members of the FRT who knew of the discovery kept it to themselves, and the purchases of the new works plates and Furness Railway number plates were discretely put on hold.

The next task for the Trust was to transport the locomotive's wheels to VSEL from storage at Carnforth. Not, it would seem, a task to daunt an organisation that had managed to get such an ambitious project under way. However, the wheels had become landlocked on an isolated piece of track, almost continuously surrounded by rakes of coaching stock. In addition to this, Steamtown's rail mounted crane was out of action. March 1997 arrived with no obvious solution to the problem and the project was starting to become seriously delayed. Frustration and outright desperation saw a gang of FRT members turn up

The engine wheels are pictured here in the Engine Shop after refurbishment by Hunslet-Barclay of Kilmarnock.
Photo: Marconi Marine

at Carnforth on the morning of Saturday 8th March with some basic equipment, including crow bars and steel channel, with which to liberate the wheels. By lunchtime, their determined efforts to move the wheels had proved successful and they arrived at VSEL the following week.

VSEL's existing working relationship with Hunslet-Barclay, the railway rolling stock manufacturers and repairers based at Kilmarnock, resulted in the wheels being sent up to Scotland in June for re-profiling and for attention to the cranks and journals. Unfortunately, the condition of the leading (plain) axle caused some concern to Hunslet-Barclay, as it appeared to be suffering from excessive corrosion. The diameter of the journals did not appear to meet modern day standards and, as an approved maintenance supplier to the railway industry, Hunslet-Barclay was reluctant to undertake the repair until this was resolved. The FRT reluctantly considered the option of replacing the plain axle until Hunslet-Barclay calculated that such a replacement would still not meet current standards. At this point, it was decided to make contact with Richard Gibbon, Head of Engineering at the National Railway Museum and the HLF's appointed monitor for the project. The FRT, after a few sleepless nights for its project committee, had concluded that this was an issue that must also have been faced by the NRM, as keeper of some of Britain's oldest locomotives. Richard immediately understood the problem and put the Trust in contact with Graham Werrett of Serco Railtest who quickly visited Kilmarnock and, after conducting successful ultrasonic tests, pronounced both axles fit for purpose. Needless to say, there was much relief all round.

Work at VSEL continued to concentrate on the overhaul of the engine chassis. Although there was little visible progress, a number of smaller cleaning and repair tasks were undertaken pending the return of the wheels. Neil Johnson had, without any luck, spent some considerable time trying to trace within VSEL a suitable machine that would accomplish the tricky task of machining the valve faces in the steam chest which had become extremely corroded. This required a mechanical planer with a reach of at least 22in. and capable of accessing an aperture of 17in.x 6in. Unfortunately, this was not a task that was to be solved quickly. It was in June of 1997 that the Trust was sorry to learn that Neil was to leave VSEL

to take up a post in the south west; Neil had been the FRT's initial point of contact and had been instrumental in getting the project under way at Barrow.

Whilst, so far, the main attention had been focused on the overhaul and repairs to the engine chassis, there was clearly a need for the FRT to make progress in the construction of the new tender. It was here that the Trust had had an amazing stroke of luck in that a photograph of the tender of an 1888 Sharp, Stewart 2-4-0 locomotive, standing forlornly on its own at the Efis Museum, Çamlik in Turkey, had been spotted by Fergus MacGregor in a copy of the Continental Railway Journal. It was already known that the engine, No.23004, was on display many miles away at Istanbul's Haydarpasa station; could the tender be purchased and brought back to England? This was a task given to Peter van Zeller who quickly managed to make contact with the appropriate authorities and also gained help from the British Embassy. Although the TCDD did, eventually, decide that the tender was part of Turkey's national heritage, the FRT's efforts were not in vain as contact was made with Alan Prior, a Briton who lived near Çamlik and who had taken the photograph. Alan readily agreed to undertake a survey of the tender and he despatched to Cumbria a full set of photographs together with a mass of detailed measurements which were to prove invaluable.

As no one had built a Sharp, Stewart tender of this design for over 100 years, its construction was obviously going to be a considerable challenge. Before his departure from VSEL, a price for the construction of the chassis had been confirmed with Neil Johnson. It had also been agreed, however, that it might be more appropriate to build the tender superstructure, with its intricate rivet detail, elsewhere. After considering several potential suppliers, Peter van Zeller suggested that an approach be made to Furness College, who had earlier indicated an interest in the project. So on Friday, 13th June, having bidden farewell to Neil in the morning, the FRT project team moved round to the Channelside complex of Furness College for a meeting with its Principal, Maggie Chadwick, Vice-Principal, Cliff Brown, and Section Head of Engineering Technology, Alastair Davidson. After confirming that the tender was to be full size (and not a model!) the response from the College was very positive as the welding and

A view of the engine chassis, with new side valances added, mounted to the refurbished wheelsets in the Engine Shop.
Photo: Furness Railway Trust

22

fabrication required would be ideal practical training for its students. The main concerns were the space required and the need for a project manager, although it was believed that solutions could be found. Maggie Chadwick promised that a decision would be made as soon as possible.

The FRT now needed to turn its attention to producing a full set of drawings for the tender. Fergus MacGregor had already put in some considerable time utilising a Computer Aided Design (CAD) package to produce drawings for new engine components and it was decided to continue to use this medium for the tender.

Alan Headech, a CRA Member from Derby, had already put in hand the production of drawings for the tender superstructure from the Sharp, Stewart outline drawings of 1863. These were to be of considerable help, together with the information to hand from Turkey, in the creation of the comprehensive computerised drawings that would be necessary for the order of individual components. Confirmation from Furness College that it was prepared to undertake the manufacture of the tender top, with its 1,200 gallons water tank and 2 tons coal capacity, put some urgency into this task. As part of the deal, the FRT agreed to pay for the costs of the College's project manager, Alan Greenwood, a former lecturer who had previously worked at the shipyard. Alan's enthusiasm and contacts at VSEL were to prove exceptionally helpful during the construction of the tender superstructure, and he quickly got to grips with the project. Alan calculated that, if timescales were to be achieved, the College would require the main sheet metal components, cut to size and bent to shape where appropriate, to be delivered to Channelside on Wednesday, 29th October, during the half term break. This would enable the staff to tack weld the main structure together in as short a time as possible. The choice of Channelside as the location for the construction of the tender tank was very appropriate, for the College's workshops had been built on the the site of the ironworks where No.7 had spent so many years of her working life.

The many hours of time necessarily spent at the computer on this project are probably the least appreciated element of input from the FRT's project team when people view the finished product. Evening after evening and weekend after weekend were spent by Fergus and the author

in studying the four Class A5 photographs that were to hand, the Sharp, Stewart drawings and the photographs from Turkey. In addition, the Trust had also gained a set of photographs of the tender of a Sharp, Stewart 0-4-2 locomotive, courtesy of the Jarnvagsmuseum, Gavle in Sweden. With so much external assistance forthcoming, there was now more of an incentive to try to achieve near perfection in the drawings. A magnifying glass was procured in order to examine the rivet detail on the 20in. x 16in. photograph of FR No.27 that had been obtained from the National Railway Museum.

The drawings were finally despatched to steel suppliers in good time to meet the timescales of Furness College and, with the assistance of VSEL, the components were duly delivered on time to the College, already bearing a coat of primer paint. VSEL had also been of great assistance in lending to the College a lifting gantry, wooden blocks, and fume extraction equipment for welding within the tank.

The shell of the tender superstructure was completed by lunchtime on Friday, 31st October, on which date the drawings for the tender chassis were delivered to Tom Jefferson, VSEL's new project manager.

Meanwhile, the author was by now taking advantage of early retirement in order to expedite the procurement of components for both the engine and tender. One item that had posed considerable problems was the manufacture of the large bell-mouthed dome. Contact with specialist metal spinners indicated that the tooling costs alone for the manufacture of this item would be over £2,000. Seeing that the FRT was now in some difficulty over the matter, Alan Middleton helpfully offered to undertake the work himself at his engineering business for a much reduced price. The finished article, skilfully manufactured out of over 50 pieces of steel, was delivered to Haverthwaite on 27th November for sanding and painting.

The extent of the project also required quite a number of both ferrous and non-ferrous castings to be produced. Fortunately, early contact was established with patternmaker Eric Clifton of Kirkham, who had formerly been in charge of a foundry and knew exactly what was required to meet the FRT's needs. Eric always managed to turn around a pattern within a week of receiving the drawings and was able to offer helpful advice on the way.

VSEL cut and assembled the chassis frames for the new tender. The chassis is shown after arrival in VSEL's Engine Shop.
Photo: Furness Railway Trust

In the knowledge that the engine's axle journals would be slightly reduced in size on their return, the first job was to replace the phosphor bronze bearings which had, in any case, become badly worn. Although only one pattern was used, it had to accommodate the surprising variations in dimensions of each of the journals and axleboxes. Thomas Sandiford of Rochdale undertook all the non-ferrous castings, and it was always a pleasure to spend half an hour there having tea with Dick Bonsor and his staff.

As the end of the year approached, however, there was still no sign of the engine's wheels arriving back at Barrow from Kilmarnock. The delays caused by the hiatus over the leading axle had pushed back timescales and, in the end, the FRT offered to arrange the transportation of the driving (crank) wheelset which was now ready at the same time as it delivered to Kilmarnock the tender wheelsets. The latter had been purchased secondhand through an advertisement in *Steam Railway* magazine and had formerly comprised the leading (smaller) wheelsets on the two snow ploughs at Buxton. Well known in the railway fraternity as *Snow King* and *Snow Queen*, these had been retired, sold and taken to Doncaster for re-use as tenders in another locomotive building project. As the smaller wheelsets were no longer required, they were ideal for the FRT being only very marginally smaller than the original Sharp, Stewart specification, and with the correct number of spokes. Originally of LNER manufacture, they possessed hefty external journals which were 6in. in diameter and much longer than required. Although the Sharp, Stewart specification was a journal diameter of only 3.5in., in line with general 19th century practice, the FRT opted for a larger 5in. diameter, which allowed room for

the machining of 0.5in. radii at both ends of each journal.

Fortunately, the FRT's Committee contained both Jim Kay Senior and Jim Kay Junior, whose family business possessed a suitable lorry for transporting wheelsets. Tuesday, 2nd December, saw a 4.00 am departure from Blackpool for Messrs. Kay and the author on a 475 miles round trip to Kilmarnock and Barrow. Despite a layer of snow that saw other HGVs despatched to the embankments of the motorways, the day was long but successful. Although two more similar round trips would eventually be necessary over the next three months to retrieve the other wheelsets, the FRT felt that meaningful progress on the vital task of getting the engine's chassis back on to its wheels could now be achieved.

Unfortunately, the optimism generated by the return of the first of the wheelsets was quickly erased with the unexpected announcement by VSEL on Friday, 12th December, that it planned to withdraw from its commercial general engineering activities. Work was expected to cease at the end of March 1998, and it was quickly confirmed by shocked VSEL staff that the future of the Class A5 project was in doubt. "Get as much completed by the end of March," was the general advice received.

On a more encouraging note, the Severn Valley Railway confirmed on 18th December that it possessed a 'home made' mechanical planing machine which was capable of machining the valve faces, and a visit to Israel Newton's workshops on 23rd December found that all three boiler rings and the firebox were now riveted together; although work was currently behind schedule, the job should be finished by the end of May 1998.

The Severn Valley Railway possesses a machine capable of planing the valve faces of inside cylinder locomotives. It is seen here in action in the Engine Shop in February 1998.
Photo: Marconi Marine

10:

Now or Never - 1998

THE FRT began 1998 with a concerted effort to complete the outstanding drawings so that as many components as possible could be manufactured by VSEL before the March deadline. Also, with timescales for both Lottery and Science Museum grants due to end in 1998, it was imperative that, wherever possible, progress be speeded up.

Saturday, 17th January, brought good news with the location at Carnforth of the original bronze valve spindle and piston rod glands. These were quickly cleaned, and all displayed the Sharp, Stewart works number *1448* as well as the order No.440. There was now no doubt that the locomotive was Furness Railway No.20, and plans were made to break the news at the FRT's Annual General Meeting on 28th March. The opportunity had also been taken to examine BHSCo. No.17, still at Carnforth. This revealed the works no.*1585* on three of the slide bar support brackets, which seemed to confirm its identity as the former Furness Railway No.25. Interestingly, though, the fourth bracket was stamped *2504*, indicating that it had been removed from BHSCo. No.23, a Sharp, Stewart 0-6-0ST built in 1875 and scrapped in 1933.

A task that had posed a significant challenge to the FRT was the tender braking system which, in line with modern regulations, had to have automatic brakes on each wheelset in order that it could be used on passenger trains. Fortunately, Trust member George Fletcher offered to accept the challenge of incorporating a vacuum brake into the design and was able to use the exercise to substantiate his (successful) application for membership of the Chartered Institute of Mechanical Engineering. Chester Wagonworks kindly offered to sell the necessary brake cylinder, which had been overhauled and certificated, and this was collected on 30th January.

Tuesday, 3rd February, saw the arrival of engineers from the Severn Valley who had brought the vital mechanical planing machine, thought to be the only example of its type in the country, in order to rectify the valve faces in the steam chest. Ironically, it is believed that the BHSCo. had, many years ago, devised a similar machine for just such purposes, and that its design had subsequently been copied by the Furness Railway, whose locomotives all had inside cylinders. The job extended over three days and was not without its difficulties. However, the finished result was a vast improvement and removed another major obstacle to restoration.

However, the future at VSEL was still clouded by the downsizing of the engineering workforce at the end of March. News came that Tom Jefferson, the second Project Manger at VSEL, would be leaving, although he was still doing his best to ensure that the project would not suffer. Work had been put in hand to manufacture the tapered cab handrails and new slide bars and there had been a test fitting in the cylinder bores of the new pistons rings. Detailed examination of the cylinder bores by VSEL staff had already confirmed that diameters varied only by a maximum of 0.025in. and that there was no need to undertake a re-bore. Reassuringly, it was learned that work was now proceeding on the new tender chassis.

The FRT, by now, needed to make a second drawdown on its Lottery grant and this precipitated a visit from Richard Gibbon in order to vet progress. Friday, 13th March, turned out to be anything but unlucky for the Trust in that Richard was more than happy with what he saw. In a whistlestop tour, he was able to inspect the work on the engine's frames, view the tender superstructure which was now ready for painting at Furness College, and then drive to Bradford to see the progress on the boiler. Highlight of the day for the FRT, however, was the first sight of the new tender chassis, which Tom Jefferson had worked especially hard to achieve for that day. Dwarfed by other ship fabrications, it was difficult at first to find it standing in the corner of the

The new boiler and firebox in the process of construction on 13th March 1998 at the Summerley Works, Bradford, of Israel Newton & Sons, Ltd.
Photo: Tim Owen

The boiler and firebox are craned off the low-loader at Haverthwaite on 16th July 1998 prior to undertaking an out-of-frames steam test later that month
Photo: Tim Owen

massive New Assembly Shop. The sight obviously made a big impact on Richard and he probably went away believing that Barrow was the Sharp, Stewart equivalent of *Jurassic Park*. With the four main elements of the project now well in hand, confirmation by Tom that day that access might be available to FRT personnel to take the project forward at VSEL workshops after the end of March was extremely heartening.

It was now clear that VSEL would be unable to undertake any more work on the project after 31st March, with only skeleton staffing being retained to service VSEL's own heavy engineering needs. The options open to the FRT were limited as previously described and, with the components of FR No.20 now liberally spread across the Engine Shop at VSEL, a move was going to be both time consuming and expensive, as well as very inconvenient. It was therefore proposed to VSEL that Alan Middleton's engineering business should take over the contract to re-assemble FR No.20, utilising VSEL's workshop facilities, with full time assistance from the author. Alan, therefore, stepped down as a FRT trustee at the AGM on 28th March, in line with Charity Commission guidelines. Having now also cleared the real identity of the locomotive with the Science Museum, the Heritage Lottery Fund and the Trust's own members, the news was made public. FR No.18 was no more; long live FR No.20!

Tuesday, 7th April, saw the start of a new era for the project when Alan and his assistant (an accountant by profession!) signed in at VSEL to start work in the Engine Shop. The first objective was to get the engine chassis back on its wheels as quickly as possible. Progress had already been made in centring the bearing brasses through the good offices of Ken Cottam, the L&HR's mechanical engineer. Ken, unfortunately, had also spotted a crack in one of the axleboxes which resulted in their all going to a specialist firm of welding engineers for an unbudgeted repair. Only after this could the new bearings be machined to fit the axleboxes.

Meanwhile, spring hangers, newly manufactured by the local forge, were fitted, the engine springs sent away for overhaul, and a variety of studs renewed on the cylinder block to enable the fitting of a new cylinder end plate. The rear cylinder covers and slide bars were fitted and the new bearing brasses scraped in.

Progress was also being made elsewhere for, after a satisfactory water test on the tender tank, performed courtesy of Barrow Fire Brigade, the new tender superstructure was handed over to the Trust on 15th May by Furness College Principal, Maggie Chadwick, and Project Manager, Alan Greenwood. This was joined in the Engine Shop on 21st May by the new tender chassis and, on that same day, the engine chassis was finally fitted on to its wheels. The day's success was tempered somewhat by the discovery that the tender wheelsets had been incorrectly machined and were 0.5in. longer than expected. Fortunately, the newly cast axleboxes had not been machined and it was subsequently found possible to compensate for this error.

The daily working party to VSEL was now being swelled on a regular basis by the addition of Brian Murray, who was on four months leave until August from his job as a Chief Engineer on a large deep sea oil tanker. Trust members Ian Camfield, John Dixon and George Fletcher also devoted some of their annual holiday to helping out at Barrow, and David Rimmer regularly made the long journey up from Liverpool to assist with the many painting and cleaning tasks. The goings on in FR No.20's bay of the huge workshop was also beginning to capture the imagination of VSEL's own staff. In particular, mention must be made of the tremendous help given by Vince Smith, a driller, who came to the FRT's assistance on many occasions, working on the project during his lunch breaks. In addition, VSEL's Ron Brown, plus Terry, Cyril and Glen, his team of crane operators, could always be relied upon to perform a lift with the 60 tons capacity overhead crane when required, and Bill Thompson would oblige by providing useful tools when needed. Despite being incomers at a time of staff redundancies, the FRT's project team was always made to feel welcome by the staff, and Kevin Brockbank, VSEL's new project manager, and Jon Wilkinson helped to ensure that everything went as smoothly as possible.

The benefits of working on the project at VSEL workshops were inestimable, once the security system had got used to the FRT's presence. Several 15 cwt capacity hoists were well located for the Trust's use for all the small lifting jobs on both the engine and tender. Air lines and

The author takes final measurements before the boiler is lowered onto the frames on Tuesday, 8th September.
Photo: Marconi Marine

tools were also made available as well as good lighting for evening work. Finally, the engine had been placed in the best spot in the Shop; right next to the tea urn!

The next milestone for the project occurred at Bradford on 15th June when the new boiler and firebox successfully passed the hydraulic test at a pressure of 240 psi. The boiler had been designed to modern standards, which assumed a maximum working pressure of 160 psi. Whilst it was not the intention of the FRT to work the boiler above 120 psi, in line with the design of the cylinders and motion, engineering practice determined that the boiler should be pumped up with water, for a very short while, to a pressure 50% greater than the design pressure.

The design of the boiler and firebox had been approved by Lloyd's Register, as part of the FRT's contract with Israel Newton & Sons. The FRT had, additionally, employed the Lakeside & Haverthwaite Railway's own insurers, Royal & Sun Alliance Engineering, to review the design in order to avoid any problems in the future. As it turned out, this had proved to be an astute move, for Royal & Sun Alliance Engineering had insisted that the boiler's longitudinal stays be augmented by four to a total of ten. In addition, the FRT had, with a view to the locomotive possibly running on Railtrack metals in its future career, asked Halcrow Transmark to examine the boiler. Representatives of all three companies, therefore, were at Newton's Summerley workshops to witness a satisfactory test, orchestrated by Halcrow Transmark's Sam Foster. The boiler works plate was then ceremonially stamped by both Lloyd's Register and Royal and Sun Alliance boiler inspectors, Jim Green and Chris Newby respectively.

Once the smokebox and ashpan had been added by Gordon Newton, the new boiler was transported to Haverthwaite on Monday, 6th July, in readiness for an out of frames steam test, which was another requirement for main line approval. The new chimney had already arrived in advance, having been manufactured by Winson Engineering of Daventry, and proved to be a perfect fit.

The annual 'Vickers' Fortnight' holiday for the shipyard's workforce, from the 24th July to 10th August, provided the opportunity for the FRT to conduct the steam test at Haverthwaite. After fitting the safety valves, gauge glasses and chimney, the first fire was lit in the grate at 12.30 pm on Wednesday, 29th July. With the steam test fixed for Friday, 31st July, there was no time to lose if the boiler and firebox was to be warmed through at a gentle pace. Although always good practice when lighting up from cold, it was all the more important to reduce stresses on the steelwork for this first steaming.

Although an air powered blower had been set up to aid air flow through the boiler tubes, it quickly became apparent that the elegant new chimney did not need much assistance. At the end of Thursday afternoon, 90 psi had been obtained with little difficulty and all looked well for the following day's test. Sam Foster arrived from Derby at 10.30 am and, with Gordon Newton in attendance, together with Jerry Bayley of Royal & Sun Alliance Engineering, steam was satisfactorily raised to 140 psi, giving an adequate safety margin over the planned working pressure.

With this important hurdle overcome, the FRT team could not wait to get back into the Engine Shop at Barrow for the final months of work that would now surely see FR No.20 steam again. Visible progress on the locomotive over the following month was rapid, with the boiler and firebox arriving at Barrow on Thursday, 20th August, the tender chassis being fitted on to its wheelsets on Wednesday, 26th August, and the boiler and firebox being successfully fitted on to the engine chassis on Tuesday, 8th September. All these events passed smoothly, but the latter gave particular cause for satisfaction as the smokebox and firebox dropped sweetly in between the frames. The smokebox had proved to be a challenge on the drawing board in that the front had to be inclined at a 5 degree angle to the vertical at the base in order to fit neatly inside the cylinder covers, a feature of the Sharp, Stewart design.

Before then, work had been completed on the valve gear, which had involved the manufacture of a new yoke, cross shaft and crank arm with which to raise and lower the Stephenson Link motion, and also the fitting of a new reach rod from the reversing lever. The chassis had been gently moved forwards and backwards along the standard gauge track in the Engine Shop to check the valve events, which appeared to be in order.

Gradually, the boiler cladding, weatherboard, cab sides and pipework were manufactured and fitted, along with the tender buffing gear and brakes. The wooden engine and tender buffer beams, provided by the same wood yard at Allithwaite that had supplied wagon underframes to the Furness Railway, were bolted to the frames and the original buffers fitted.

A layer of keruing hardwood, to act as a cushion, was fitted to the top of the tender frames in line with traditional practice and the superstructure was finally lowered on to the frames on Friday, 4th, December. At the same time, the opportunity was taken to fit the large dome cover on the engine. At last, both engine and tender now looked ready for business, but there was still a great deal of work to be completed before the first steaming just over a month away. Much to the disappointment of VSEL's Engine Shop

workforce, the decision was taken for practical reasons at this juncture to have the first steaming of the locomotive at Haverthwaite, the locomotive's new home, rather than at Barrow. With the Heritage Lottery Fund's grant timescale due to expire at the end of January, a move to Haverthwaite before Christmas would enable work to continue during the shipyard's holiday period.

In order to have the locomotive on view to FRT members at the weekend of the L&HR's Father Christmas special trains, a removal date of Thursday, 17th December, was fixed. At this point, all the outstanding jobs were listed and a painting programme devised which would see the locomotive delivered in its full Indian Red livery.

Local historian Phil Cousins joined the team to assist in painting and, with Brian Murray back from the sea, working hours extended well into the evening in order to ensure

The tender arrives at
Haverthwaite on Thursday,
17th December, 1998.
Photo: Tim Owen

that deadlines were achieved. This, incidently, was welcomed by the VSEL nightshift who were pleased to have some company during the dark winter evenings.

With assembly almost complete and painting well under way, it was now possible to begin to compare the locomotive outline with those portrayed by the four photographs. Immediately apparent was the rich colour of the Indian Red paint which, with the brasswork and extensive black and vermilion lining, contrasted greatly with the black and grey tones previously seen on the black and white photographs. Although some reference books had recorded that the Furness Railway Class A5 locomotives were painted black, close examination of the shading on the black and white photographs available clearly showed that this was, at least, untrue for Nos. 27 and 28. The FRT had needed little persuasion, therefore, to adopt the Furness Red colour for FR No.20.

The photographs of FR Nos.27 and 28 had also showed that new sandboxes had been fitted during their lives, and that a cylinder lubricator had been mounted behind the chimney. The decision had been taken by the project team to fit sandboxes to No.20 which were in line with the original drawings, whilst it was also decided, for the immediate future, to rely on the original lubrication system which consisted of brass tallow cocks located on the valve chest and cylinder covers. A weatherboard had been fitted to the tender, in line with photographs of FR No.27, and this was believed to be prototypical for locomotives working on lines without a turntable at each end.

On Friday afternoon, 11th December, Ron Brown set about the delicate task of moving the engine on to the rails, conveniently set into the floor of the main shop passageway, from which it could be loaded on to a transporter the following week. Well out of sight of the eyes of the rest of the workforce, who had gone home, two large spreading beams were hung beneath the 60 tons overhead crane and the engine was slowly and carefully raised into the air, perfectly balanced. There was relief all round when the wheels touched down, and the procedure was successfully repeated with the tender the following Monday morning.

One of the last tasks was to fit the tender springs, which could only be undertaken after the tank had been painted.

This was finally completed on Tuesday, 15th December, coincident with a visit from Jerry Bayley of Royal & Sun Alliance Engineering to undertake a dry inspection of the boiler. A provisional steam test date of 13th January was fixed.

Time was also spent in fitting the final embellishments such as the works plates, number plates and brass numerals on the buffer beams. Considerable research and care had been taken to try and ensure that these were as authentic in appearance as possible. In contrast with the 19th century technology that had built the locomotive, rubbings from an original Sharp Stewart works plate had been scanned into a computer and the numbers altered to suit. The data had then been downloaded on to a disc which was afterwards sent to a specialist engraving firm for reproduction in brass. Photographs of various Furness Railway locomotives had been examined to aid the design of the curved brass number plates and also to assist in the positioning of the screw holes for the buffer beam numerals. A final touch had been the manufacture of two replica locomotive lamps. Since no existing FR lamps had been located, the FRT had requested John Beesley, a specialist in producing such railway items, to construct new lamps with square pintles from enlargements of photographs provided by local railway historian Geoff Holme.

With painting completed to schedule on Wednesday, 16th December, the only outstanding item that had failed to materialise was the decorative brass cladding between the boiler and firebox. This, again, was a specialist job that was eventually accomplished in January by a professional vintage car restorer. However, in order to cover the gap for the locomotive's first appearance to the public, Phil made a very creditable temporary job (which fooled many people) out of seasonal gold gift wrap and some black tape, complete with vermilion lining!

Thursday, 17th December, saw the FRT team start to assemble in the Engine Shop at 7.20 am. With special permission granted to take photographs, the historic scene was well documented. Small posses of VSEL staff had been passing through the Shop during the last few days to view the locomotive before it departed; word was obviously

Back on former Furness Railway Metals. FR No.20 is unloaded at Haverthwaite on 17th December 1998.
Photo: Tim Owen

Basking in the winter sunshine, the completed locomotive.
Photo: Alan Middleton

passing about the Yard and still more staff were to be found that morning, paying their last respects and admiring the finished paintwork. The specialist low loader arrived at 8.35 am and the tender was loaded without difficulty.

Arrival at Haverthwaite was greeted by a gathering of FRT members who had come to see the fruits of the project team's labours. At last, despite the greyness of the clouded skies, the true beauty of the lined out Indian Red livery could be appreciated. After unloading, the transporter promptly returned to Barrow and swiftly loaded the engine. Unlike the traditional launch of a ship, little ceremony had been planned for the emergence from the works of the locomotive. However, the promise of the first sighting of a Furness Railway Class A5 locomotive for eighty years

had proved to be an occasion not to be missed by local railway enthusiasts. With the local press also alerted to this historic event, a crowd of interested spectators had gathered at the Traffic Gate entrance to the works in Bridge Road. All eyes were straining as the shiny red engine, brasswork gleaming, approached the gates. There was a pause whilst photographs were taken for the record before the ensemble moved off towards Haverthwaite.

Even more people had gathered to form a welcoming party at Haverthwaite and, at 3.00 pm, the engine was finally re-united with former Furness Railway metals. At 3.50 pm, the engine and tender were successfully paired up for the first time and the locomotive moved to pride of place in the engine shed.

Trial running of FR No.20 on the bank at Backbarrow on the Lakeside & Haverthwaite Railway on Tuesday, 9th February 1999.

Photo: Tim Owen

11:
Steaming Again - 1999

Alan Middleton holds the umbrella for Lady Grania Cavendish during the ceremony at Haverthwaite to mark the introduction into service of the restored locomotive on 20th April 1999. Tim Owen (left) and John Dixon look on.

Photo: Ken Royall

FRIDAY, 8th January, saw Furness Railway locomotive No.20 drawn out of Haverthwaite engine shed, well out of sight of the main road. On that cold but bright winter's morning, four people, Alan Middleton, Peter van Zeller, Brian Murray and the author, had gathered to undertake a test steaming of the locomotive in preparation for the official steam test the following Wednesday.

The fire was quickly lit and was again drawn strongly by the new chimney, with barely any smoke emanating from the firehole door. Three hours soon passed as the gang busied themselves with polishing the brasswork and oiling up the motion. At last, the pressure gauge showed signs of movement and the new four hole blower quickly took hold of the fire. Pressure gradually rose to around seventy pounds, at which point Alan had had enough of the waiting. Would it move? We were quickly to find out as the regulator was opened up further and further until, in a flurry of steam issuing from the cylinder and valve chest steam cocks, the locomotive eased gently forward.

In an instant, all the private fears and concerns about whether the engine had been re-assembled correctly from that incomplete kit of parts disappeared. Here was a working engine; not only did it move evenly forwards and backwards, but the injectors operated smoothly and the clack valves proved to be free of any leaks. In fact, apart from some persistent passing of steam through the regulator, it was difficult to find fault.

With confidence rapidly in the ascendant, FR No.20 moved round into the main yard under her own steam, to be spotted by passing motorists, many of whom could hardly believe their own eyes. Basking there in the winter sun was a most glorious sight to behold, the paintwork and brass glinting, and the piercing steam whistle sending a shiver down the spine of all those who stood and watched. FR No.20 was again alive and well!

The weather turned extremely cold that weekend, and a warming fire was placed in the engine on Monday, 11th January, much to the delight of Chris Dixon, Northern News Editor of *Railway World*, who seized his chance, in perfect light conditions, to take the cover photograph for the next issue.

News of the exciting events at Haverthwaite spread swiftly and brought with it a request from the BBC to film the official steam test on Wednesday, 13th January. With the station yard now covered with a thick layer of ice, and all concerned braving the sleet and snow in the open cab, FR No.20 successfully passed her steam test and then proceeded to haul a four-wheeled LMS 20 ton brake van on an inaugural trip to Lakeside. The BBC team put together a fine piece of film for the evening's local news programme and the event also received widespread coverage on local radio and on Ceefax. Imagine the tremendous glow of satisfaction felt the following day on gaining sight of the local newspaper hoardings proclaiming 'Loco Steams

Again'. Yes, the people of Furness had taken FR No.20 to their hearts. Once again, they had a Furness Railway locomotive of their own to replace *Coppernob*.

This, however, was just the beginning. The locomotive took the railway press by storm for, with the tight security in place at VSEL, little had been published about the restoration that was taking place behind closed doors. The procession of people visiting the engine shed at Haverthwaite also told its own story; many were heard to ask where the engine had been hiding all these years, whilst quite a few reminisced about happy hours playing on it during its time in the school playground in Barrow.

Proving trials over the next month again showed the only major problem to be the leaking regulator, which showed no signs of improvement, and there was a propensity for the engine to issue an embarrassing amount of dirty water, much to the discomfort of the enginemen! The locomotive, though, showed every signs of steaming well and a press launch was fixed for Tuesday, 20th April, followed by a first public steaming for FRT/LRS members the following Sunday. In preparation for this, the locomotive's vacuum brake system had been commissioned and, on Wednesday, 14th April, two Mark 1 coaches were hauled for the first time. After a successful test run up the bank, the locomotive then took the place of the L&HR's diesel multiple unit in operating a special 3.00 pm public train from Haverthwaite, and returning with a pre-booked party of foreign tourists from Lakeside, much to their delight!

The press launch was, apart from dreadful weather, another success for FR No.20. Guest of Honour at the ceremony to commission the locomotive into service was Lady Grania Cavendish, whose husband's family had been prominent promoters of the Furness Railway in the 1840s. Other guests included many who were representing businesses which had manufactured and repaired components for the locomotive. The guests were hauled on a return trip to Lakeside, including a memorable run past by the train at Newby Bridge, and the ceremony was broadcast live on BBC 'Radio Cumbria'.

The public steaming on 25th April, when FR No.20 hauled three return trips double-heading with the FRT's appropriately Furness Railway liveried 'Austerity' 0-6-0ST *Cumbria*, brought hundreds of people to Haverthwaite, including enthusiasts who had travelled many miles to see this remarkable old engine back in steam.

The FRT could not have wished for a better conclusion to the project and it was a delight for all concerned to receive the seal of approval from Richard Gibbon, Head of Engineering at the National Railway Museum and the Heritage Lottery Fund's project monitor. All the grant monies had, by now, been successfully claimed and the FRT's Committee could at last afford to relax a little. The project had eventually cost £140,000, which was £10,000 (8%) more than the original budget, but this was generally thought to be acceptable bearing in mind the nature of the task.

The only major outstanding issues now to be resolved were the leaking regulator valve and excessive water consumption, which were adversely affecting coal consumption. The matter was finally brought to a head on 3rd May when, whilst again double-heading with 'Cumbria', an excess of water in the right hand cylinder caused the rear cylinder cover joint to fail. The locomotive was immediately taken out of traffic and, after the cylinder cover joint had been repaired, the dome was removed to allow inspection of the regulator. A simple test with a hose pipe confirmed the FRT's belief that the joint between the regulator valve 'J'-pipe and the main steam pipe had failed, possibly imploding during the hydraulic test the previous June. Repairs were carried out over the following month and the locomotive steamed again on Monday, 14th June, hauling three Mark 1 carriages to Lakeside on two return trips during the evening. This time, there was not a wisp of steam to be seen when the regulator was shut and no water had passed through into the cylinders.

With the confidence that this problem had been overcome, it was then decided to advertise a series of five Tuesday evening special trains on the L&HR in August, to be hauled by FR No. 20, which would help to build up her operational mileage. To the delight of all concerned, public response exceeded expectations, with people travelling hundreds of miles to travel behind this special locomotive. Although it was only intended to operate the trains with two Mark 1 carriages, an additional coach had to be added on the 24th August; the train, grossing 110 tons, was handled without fuss by FR No. 20, despite the steep gradient out of Haverthwaite station.

What Now for FR No.20?

The locomotive has now taken on the mantle of being the oldest working standard gauge steam locomotive in Britain, and one of the oldest steamable locomotives in the world. Her home at Haverthwaite is undoubtedly appropriate, particularly since it is quite likely that FR No.20 was used to haul construction materials for the Lakeside Branch, which was opened on 1st June 1869, a year before FR No.20 was sold to the Barrow Haematite Steel Co. She is now able to steam leisurely to Lakeside to meet up with another much loved Furness Railway legacy, the lake steamer *Tern* built in 1891.

FR No.20's fame has already spread far and wide, and it is planned that she will appear at the prestigious Millennium Cavalcade of Steam in the year 2000 to commemorate the 175th anniversary of the opening of the Stockton and Darlington Railway. But what does the future hold for FR No.20? It is to be hoped that the 1998 rebuild will now give the locomotive a new lease of life that will see her steaming well into the new millennium, giving pleasure and understanding of early railway design to generations to come. However, it is surely unlikely that FR No.20's future career could be anything like as remarkable as the first 136 years of her life!

COVER PHOTOGRAPHS

Front Cover:
FR No. 20 heads the 10.35 hrs. train from Haverthwaite to Lakeside up Backbarrow bank on Monday, 3rd May 1999
Photo: Phil Cousins

Back Cover:
FR No.20 pauses beneath the footbridge at Haverthwaite during trial running on the Lakeside & Haverthwaite Railway on Wednesday, 10th February 1999
Photo: Peter van Campenhout